CASTING CROWNS
THE VERY NEXT THING

ISBN 978-1-4950-7469-1

7777 W. BLUEMOUND RD. P.O. BOX 13819 MILWAUKEE, WI 53213

In Australia Contact:
Hal Leonard Australia Pty. Ltd.
4 Lentara Court
Cheltenham, Victoria, 3192 Australia
Email: ausadmin@halleonard.com.au

Visit Hal Leonard Online at
www.halleonard.com

HALLELUJAH

Words and Music by JOHN MARK HALL,
BERNIE HERMS and GRIFFIN KELP

Powerfully, with praise

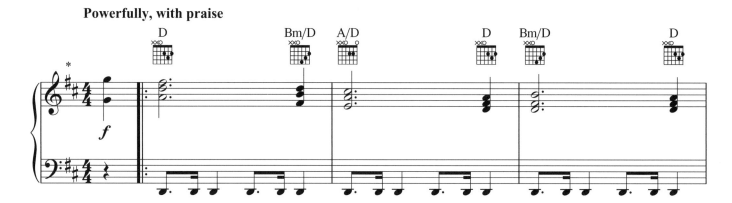

On the morn-ing of ___ cre - a - tion,

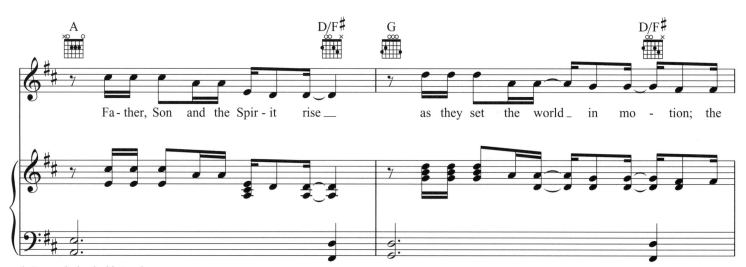

Fa - ther, Son and the Spir - it rise ___ as they set the world ___ in mo - tion; the

* *Recorded a half step lower.*

To Coda ⊕

THE VERY NEXT THING

Words and Music by MATTHEW WEST,
JOHN MARK HALL and BERNIE HERMS

Moderate Rock beat

I spend all my _

_ time dream - ing what the fu - ture's gon-na bring when all of this

time there's a world _ pass - ing by right in front of me. Set my sights on to -

* Recorded a half step higher.

ONE STEP AWAY

Words and Music by MATTHEW WEST,
BERNIE HERMS and JOHN MARK HALL

Recorded a half step lower.

OH MY SOUL

Words and Music by JOHN MARK HALL
and BERNIE HERMS

WHAT IF I GAVE EVERYTHING

Words and Music by MATTHEW WEST,
JOHN MARK HALL and BERNIE HERMS

GOD OF ALL MY DAYS

Words and Music by JOHN MARK HALL
and JASON INGRAM

* Recorded a half step lower.

WHEN THE GOD-MAN PASSES BY

Words and Music by JOHN MARK HALL
and BERNIE HERMS

* Recorded a half step lower.

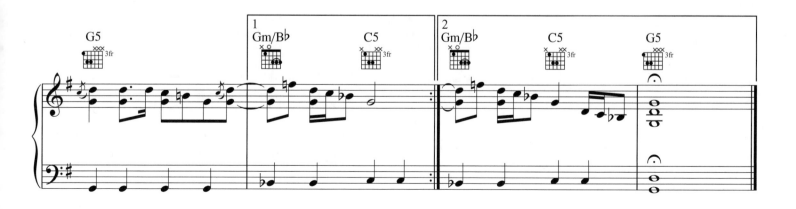

FOR ALL YOU ARE

Words and Music by JOHN MARK HALL,
JASON INGRAM and ZACH WELLIVER

SONG THAT THE ANGELS CAN'T SING

Words and Music by
MEGAN GARRETT

A
E
F♯m
D
-jah to the Lamb that was slain. Well, I can-not hold it in;
A
E
D
You've giv-en me a brand-new name. A song of my de-liv-
A
E
F♯m
D
-er-ance: You've bro-ken all my chains and I am free.
E
A
Oh, I have a song the an-gels can't sing.

MAKE ME A RIVER

Words and Music by MATTHEW WEST
and JOHN MARK HALL

NO OTHER NAME

Words and Music by JOEL HOUSTON
and JONAS MYRIN

LOVING MY JESUS

Words and Music by MATTHEW WEST
and JOHN MARK HALL

Gentle Ballad, in a slow 2

I was a wan - d'ring
make you

soul, trav - 'ling a well - worn
hide, whis - pers that same old

road,_____ a sin - ner so
lie:_____ keep all your

far from home,_____ no sec - ond chance in
pain in - side,_____ 'cause no one will un - der -

* *Recorded a half step lower.*

Contemporary Christian Artist Folios from Hal Leonard
Arranged for Piano, Voice and Guitar

CASTING CROWNS – THRIVE
All the tracks from this popular Christian band's 2014 album, including the lead single "All You've Ever Wanted," plus: Broken Together • Dream for You • Follow Me • House of Their Dreams • Just Be Held • Thrive • and more.
00125333 P/V/G.............$16.99

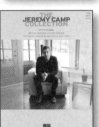

THE JEREMY CAMP COLLECTION
A collection of 21 of this Dove Award-winner's best, including: Empty Me • Healing Hand of God • Jesus Saves • Let It Fade • Right Here • Stay • Take You Back • Walk by Faith • and more.
00307200 P/V/G.............$17.99

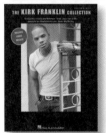

THE KIRK FRANKLIN COLLECTION
16 of Kirk Franklin's most popular gospel hits: Declaration (This Is It) • Help Me Believe • I Smile • Lean on Me • Looking for You • Jesus • Now Behold the Lamb • Stomp • Whatcha Lookin' 4? • Why We Sing • and more.
00307222 P/V/G.............$17.99

THE VERY BEST OF HILLSONG
25 songs from the popular worldwide church including: Came to My Rescue • From the Inside Out • Hosanna • I Give You My Heart • Lead Me to the Cross • Mighty to Save • Shout to the Lord • The Stand • Worthy Is the Lamb • and more.
00312101 P/V/G.............$17.99

HILLSONG MODERN WORSHIP HITS
20 songs, including: Alive • Broken Vessels (Amazing Grace) • Christ Is Enough • Cornerstone • Forever Reign • God Is Able • Mighty to Save • The Stand • This I Believe (The Creed) • Touch the Sky • and more.
00154952 P/V/G.............$16.99

HILLSONG UNITED – EMPIRES
A dozen songs from the "Empires" collection by top Christian artists who have performed at Australia's Hillsong Church: Closer Than You Know • Empires • Heart like Heaven • Here Now (Madness) • and more.
00156715 P/V/G.............$16.99

KARI JOBE – WHERE I FIND YOU
12 songs from Jobe's sophomore CD: Find You on My Knees • Here • Love Came Down • One Desire • Rise • Run to You (I Need You) • Savior's Here • Stars in the Sky • Steady My Heart • We Are • We Exalt Your Name • What Love Is This.
00307381 P/V/G......................$16.99

THE BEST OF MERCYME
20 of the best from these Texan Christian rockers, including: All of Creation • Beautiful • Bring the Rain • God with Us • Here with Me • Homesick • The Hurt and the Healer • I Can Only Imagine • Move • Word of God Speak • and more.
00118899 P/V/G.............$17.99

MERCYME – WELCOME TO THE NEW
This 2014 album reached #1 on the Billboard® Top Christian Album charts and as high as #4 on the Billboard® 200 album charts. Our matching songbook includes all ten tracks from the CD: Burn Baby Burn • Flawless • Greater • New Lease on Life • Shake • Welcome to the New • and more.
00128518 P/V/G......................$16.99

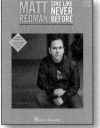

THE BEST OF PASSION
Over 40 worship favorites featuring the talents of David Crowder, Matt Redman, Chris Tomlin, and others. Songs include: Always • Awakening • Blessed Be Your Name • Here for You • How Marvelous • Jesus Paid It All • My Heart Is Yours • Our God • 10,000 Reasons (Bless the Lord) • You Are My King (Amazing Love) • and more.
00101888 P/V/G......................$19.99

MATT REDMAN – SING LIKE NEVER BEFORE: THE ESSENTIAL COLLECTION
Our matching folio features 15 songs, including "10,000 Reasons (Bless the Lord)" and: Better Is One Day • The Father's Song • The Heart of Worship • Love So High • Nothing but the Blood • and more.
00116963 P/V/G......................$16.99

SWITCHFOOT – THE BEST YET
This greatest hits compilation features the newly released song "This Is Home" and 17 other top songs. Includes: Concrete Girl • Dare You to Move • Learning to Breathe • Meant to Live • Only Hope • Stars • and more.
00307030 P/V/G.............$17.99

TENTH AVENUE NORTH – THE LIGHT MEETS THE DARK
The very latest from this Florida CCM band contains 11 songs, the hit single "You Are More" and: All the Pretty Things • Any Other Way • Empty My Hands • Healing Begins • House of Mirrors • Oh My Dear • On and On • Strong Enough to Save • The Truth Is Who You Are.
00307148 P/V/G......................$16.99

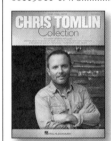

THIRD DAY – LEAD US BACK: SONGS OF WORSHIP
All 12 tracks from Third Day's first collection of all-orginal worship songs: Father of Lights • He Is Alive • I Know You Can • In Jesus Name • Lead Us Back • Maker • The One I Love • Our Deliverer • Soul on Fire • Spirit • Victorious • Your Words.
00145263 P/V/G......................$16.99

CHRIS TOMLIN – BURNING LIGHTS
A dozen songs from the 2013 release from this Christian songwriting giant! Includes the lead single "Whom Shall I Fear (God of Angel Armies)" plus: Awake My Soul • Countless Wonders • God's Great Dance Floor • Lay Me Down • Sovereign • and more.
00115644 P/V/G......................$16.99

THE CHRIS TOMLIN COLLECTION – 2ND EDITION
This second edition features a fresh mix of 15 Tomlin favorites, including: Amazing Grace (My Chains Are Gone) • Forever • Holy Is the Lord • How Great Is Our God • Jesus Loves Me • Jesus Messiah • Our God • Waterfall • We Fall Down • and more.
00306951 P/V/G......................$16.99

CHRIS TOMLIN – LOVE RAN RED
Matching piano/vocal/guitar arrangements to Tomlin's 2014 release featuring 12 tracks: Almighty • At the Cross (Love Ran Red) • Fear Not • Greater • Jesus Loves Me • The Roar • Waterfall • and more.
00139166 P/V/G.............$16.99

THE BEST OF MATTHEW WEST
16 top singles from popular Christian artist Matthew West arranged for piano, voice and guitar. Includes: Do Something • Forgiveness • Grace Wins • Mended • Only Grace • Strong Enough • When I Say I Do • You Are Everything • and more.
00159489 P/V/G......................$16.99

HAL•LEONARD®

For a complete listing of the products we have available, visit us online at www.halleonard.com

0916